Francis Frith's
SHEFFIELD AND SOUTH YORKSHIRE

PHOTOGRAPHIC MEMORIES

Francis Frith's
SHEFFIELD
AND SOUTH YORKSHIRE

◆

Clive Hardy

First published in the United Kingdom in 1999 by
Frith Book Company Ltd

British Library Cataloguing in Publication Data

Sheffield and South Yorkshire
Clive Hardy
ISBN 1-85937-070-5

Frith Book Company Ltd
Frith's Barn, Teffont,
Salisbury, Wiltshire SP3 5QP
Tel: +44 (0) 1722 716 376
Email: frithbook.co.uk

Printed and bound in Great Britain

CONTENTS

FRANCIS FRITH: *Victorian Pioneer*

FRANCIS FRITH, Victorian founder of the world-famous photographic archive, was a complex and multitudinous man. A devout Quaker and a highly successful Victorian businessman, he was both philosophic by nature and pioneering in outlook.

By 1855 Francis Frith had already established a wholesale grocery business in Liverpool, and sold it for the astonishing sum of £200,000, which is the equivalent today of over £15,000,000. Now a multi-millionaire, he was able to indulge his passion for travel. As a child he had pored over travel books written by early explorers, and his fancy and imagination had been stirred by family holidays to the sublime mountain regions of Wales and Scotland. 'What a land of spirit-stirring and enriching scenes and places!' he had written. He was to return to these scenes of grandeur in later years to 'recapture the thousands of vivid and tender memories', but with a different purpose. Now in his thirties, and captivated by the new science of photography, Frith set out on a series of pioneering journeys to the Nile regions that occupied him from 1856 until 1860.

INTRIGUE AND ADVENTURE

He took with him on his travels a specially-designed wicker carriage that acted as both dark-room and sleeping chamber. These far-flung journeys were packed with intrigue and adventure. In his life story, written when he was sixty-three, Frith tells of being held captive by bandits, and of fighting 'an awful midnight battle to the very point of surrender with a deadly pack of hungry, wild dogs'. Sporting flowing Arab costume, Frith arrived at Akaba by camel seventy years before Lawrence, where he encountered 'desert princes and rival sheikhs, blazing with jewel-hilted swords'.

During these extraordinary adventures he was assiduously exploring the desert regions bordering the Nile and patiently recording the antiquities and peoples with his camera. He was the first photographer to venture beyond the sixth cataract. Africa was still the mysterious 'Dark Continent', and Stanley and Livingstone's historic meeting was a decade into the future. The conditions for picture taking confound belief. He laboured for hours in his wicker dark-room in the sweltering heat of the desert, while the volatile chemicals fizzed dangerously in their trays. Often he was forced to work in remote tombs and caves

where conditions were cooler. Back in London he exhibited his photographs and was 'rapturously cheered' by members of the Royal Society. His reputation as a photographer was made overnight. An eminent modern historian has likened their impact on the population of the time to that on our own generation of the first photographs taken on the surface of the moon.

VENTURE OF A LIFE-TIME

Characteristically, Frith quickly spotted the opportunity to create a new business as a specialist publisher of photographs. He lived in an era of immense and sometimes violent change. For the poor in the early part of Victoria's reign work was a drudge and the hours long, and people had precious little free time to enjoy themselves.

Most had no transport other than a cart or gig at their disposal, and had not travelled far beyond the boundaries of their own town or village. However, by the 1870s, the railways had threaded their way across the country, and Bank Holidays and half-day Saturdays had been made obligatory by Act of Parliament. All of a sudden the ordinary working man and his family were able to enjoy days out and see a little more of the world.

With characteristic business acumen, Francis Frith foresaw that these new tourists would enjoy having souvenirs to commemorate their days out. In 1860 he married Mary Ann Rosling and set out with the intention of photographing every city, town and village in Britain. For the next thirty years he travelled the country by train and by pony and trap, producing fine photographs of seaside resorts and beauty spots that were keenly bought by millions of Victorians. These prints were painstakingly pasted into family albums and pored over during the dark nights of winter, rekindling precious memories of summer excursions.

THE RISE OF FRITH & CO

Frith's studio was soon supplying retail shops all over the country. To meet the demand he gathered about him a small team of photographers, and published the work of independent artist-photographers of the calibre of Roger Fenton and Francis Bedford. In order to gain some understanding of the scale of Frith's business one only has to look at the catalogue issued by Frith & Co in 1886: it runs to some 670

pages, listing not only many thousands of views of the British Isles but also many photographs of most European countries, and China, Japan, the USA and Canada – note the sample page shown above from the hand-written *Frith & Co* ledgers detailing pictures taken. By 1890 Frith had created the greatest specialist photographic publishing company in the world, with over 2,000 outlets – more than the combined number that Boots and WH Smith have today! The picture on the right shows the *Frith & Co* display board at Ingleton in the Yorkshire Dales. Beautifully constructed with mahogany frame and gilt inserts, it could display up to a dozen local scenes.

POSTCARD BONANZA

◆◆

The ever-popular holiday postcard we know today took many years to develop. In 1870 the Post Office issued the first plain cards, with a pre-printed stamp on one face. In 1894 they allowed other publishers' cards to be sent through the mail with an attached adhesive halfpenny stamp. Demand grew rapidly, and in 1895 a new size of postcard was permitted called the

court card, but there was little room for illustration. In 1899, a year after Frith's death, a new card measuring 5.5 x 3.5 inches became the standard format, but it was not until 1902 that the divided back came into being, with address and message on one face and a full-size illustration on the other. *Frith & Co* were in the vanguard of postcard development, and Frith's sons Eustace and Cyril continued their father's monumental task, expanding the number of views offered to the public and recording more and more places in Britain, as the coasts and countryside were opened up to mass travel.

Francis Frith died in 1898 at his villa in Cannes, his great project still growing. The archive he created continued in business for another seventy years. By 1970 it contained over a third of a million pictures of 7,000 cities, towns and villages. The massive photographic record Frith has left to us stands as a living monument to a special and very remarkable man.

Frith's Archive: *A Unique Legacy*

FRANCIS FRITH'S legacy to us today is of immense significance and value, for the magnificent archive of evocative photographs he created provides a unique record of change in 7,000 cities, towns and villages throughout Britain over a century and more. Frith and his fellow studio photographers revisited locations many times down the years to update their views, compiling for us an enthralling and colourful pageant of British life and character.

We tend to think of Frith's sepia views of Britain as nostalgic, for most of us use them to conjure up memories of places in our own lives with which we have family associations. It often makes us forget that to Francis Frith they were records of daily life as it was actually being lived in the cities, towns and villages of his day. The Victorian age was one of great and often bewildering change for ordinary people, and though the pictures evoke an impression of slower times, life was as busy and hectic as it is today.

We are fortunate that Frith was a photographer of the people, dedicated to recording the minutiae of everyday life. For it is this sheer wealth of visual data, the painstaking chronicle of changes in dress, transport, street layouts, buildings, housing, engineering and landscape that captivates us so much today. His remarkable images offer us a powerful link with the past and with the lives of our ancestors.

TODAY'S TECHNOLOGY

Computers have now made it possible for Frith's many thousands of images to be accessed almost instantly. In the Frith archive today, each photograph is carefully 'digitised' then stored on a CD Rom. Frith archivists can locate a single photograph amongst thousands within seconds. Views can be catalogued and sorted under a variety of categories of place and content to the immediate benefit of researchers. Inexpensive reference prints can be created for them at the touch of a mouse button, and a wide range of books and other printed materials assembled and published for a wider, more general readership - in the next twelve months over a hundred Frith local history titles will be published! The

See Frith at www. francisfrith.co.uk

day-to-day workings of the archive are very different from how they were in Francis Frith's time: imagine the herculean task of sorting through eleven tons of glass negatives as Frith had to do to locate a particular sequence of pictures! Yet the archive still prides itself on maintaining the same high standards of excellence laid down by Francis Frith, including the painstaking cataloguing and indexing of every view.

It is curious to reflect on how the internet now allows researchers in America and elsewhere greater instant access to the archive than Frith himself ever enjoyed. Many thousands of individual views can be called up on screen within seconds on one of the Frith internet sites, enabling people living continents away to revisit the streets of their ancestral home town, or view places in Britain where they have enjoyed holidays. Many overseas researchers welcome the chance to view special theme selections, such as transport, sports, costume and ancient monuments.

We are certain that Francis Frith would have heartily approved of these modern developments, for he himself was always working at the very limits of Victorian photographic technology.

THE VALUE OF THE ARCHIVE TODAY

Because of the benefits brought by the computer, Frith's images are increasingly studied by social historians, by researchers into genealogy and ancestory, by architects, town planners, and by teachers and schoolchildren involved in local history projects. In addition, the archive offers every one of us a unique opportunity to examine the places where we and our families have lived and worked down the years. Immensely successful in Frith's own era, the archive is now, a century and more on, entering a new phase of popularity.

THE PAST IN TUNE WITH THE FUTURE

Historians consider the Francis Frith Collection to be of prime national importance. It is the only archive of its kind remaining in private ownership and has been valued at a million pounds. However, this figure is now rapidly increasing as digital technology enables more and more people around the world to enjoy its benefits.

Francis Frith's archive is now housed in an historic timber barn in the beautiful village of Teffont in Wiltshire. Its founder would not recognize the archive office as it is today. In place of the many thousands of dusty boxes containing glass plate negatives and an all-pervading odour of photographic chemicals, there are now ranks of computer screens. He would be amazed to watch his images travelling round the world at unimaginable speeds through network and internet lines.

The archive's future is both bright and exciting. Francis Frith, with his unshakeable belief in making photographs available to the greatest number of people, would undoubtedly approve of what is being done today with his lifetime's work. His photographs, depicting our shared past, are now bringing pleasure and enlightenment to millions around the world a century and more after his death.

SHEFFIELD – *An Introduction*

In 1974 the Local Government Act 1972 came into effect; with it a came a radical realignment of many of our county boundaries, with scant regard for history, tradition, community or identity. Southern Lancashire was butchered to create the Metropolitan Boroughs of Merseyside and Greater Manchester; Cumberland and Westmorland were abolished altogether; Rutland, England's smallest county, was dragged kicking and screaming into a merger with Leicestershire; Yorkshire, the largest county, was dissected. The provisions of the Act saw the abolition of the three Ridings, an administrative division that had served the county well for nearly a thousand years. Their place was taken by three new counties, North Yorkshire, South Yorkshire and West Yorkshire. In addition former East and West Riding territory was hived off to create something called Humberside; Lancashire and the new county of Cumbria gained parts of the western areas of the West Riding, and a part of the North Riding which included the great steel town of Middlesbrough was incorporated into the new county of Cleveland.

When South Yorkshire came into being, it was still an industrial powerhouse founded on coal, steelmaking and heavy industry centred on Sheffield, Rotherham, Doncaster and Barnsley. Twenty-five years on, things have changed. True, Sheffield is still a major steelmaking area; but it no longer provides employment on a massive scale. Coal mining paid the price for taking on the Thatcher Government in 1984. After a strike lasting just under a year, the miners were back at work with nothing to show for their stand. Retribution came in the form of closures, including profitable or potentially profitable pits; and as the remaining collieries were privatised, the NCB ceased to exist.

The earliest pictures of this area in the Frith Collection were taken in Sheffield around 1870. By this time the town's population was approaching the 240,000 mark; it would reach 284,000 in 1881, and by the beginning of the 20th century it would be over 400,000. Throughout much of the 19th century boom would follow bust for Sheffield's industries, and in 1878, though the town was experiencing the fastest population growth of any provincial town, local industry was feeling the effects of yet another slump. Brown Bailey, Midland Iron, Sheffield Forge & Rolling Mills, the Sheffield Patent Brick Co and the Yorkshire Engine Co were just a few of the firms to lay off workers and declare that they were unable to pay any dividends to their shareholders.

By the time the Frith cameraman visited Sheffield again in 1893, major changes were taking place in the town centre, possibly in connection with it being made a city. The development had begun in the 1840s when

ber is that the Frith cameraman's brief would be to take photographs of subjects considered suitable for publication as postcards, rather than for their social or historical value. By the 1890s postcards were beginning to catch on with the public, even though the cards had to be placed inside an envelope for posting. In 1894 the Post Office had a change of policy and allowed postcards to be sent without an envelope for half the normal letter rate, though only the address of the recipient

the Town Trustees began getting involved in road-widening schemes, including those at Snig Hill, Tenter Street, Trippet Lane, and Figtree Lane. In 1875 the town centre was redeveloped with the construction of Pinstone Street, Leopold Street and Surrey Street, and in 1893 the Council began a slum clearance programme in the Crofts, an area extending from the rear of the parish church to West Bar. Plans were drawn up for the erection of a new Town Hall befitting the newest city in the kingdom. Our cameraman also paid a visit to the city's parks, the Ruskin Museum which had moved to Meersbrook House a couple of years earlier, and the Mappin Art Gallery. What we have to remem-

could be written on them. It was not until 1902 that you were allowed to write a message; since then millions of cards have been written to say 'having a wonderful time, the weather is lovely'.

Frith sent a cameraman to Sheffield in 1896 to take pictures of the recently completed Town Hall, and further visits were made in 1900 and 1902. There was then a gap of nearly fifty years before photographs were taken of the city centre, the university and several parks, with a follow-up session in the mid to late 1960s. The pictures from c1955 capture something of the rebuilding and redevelopment of the city centre following the heavy damage inflicted upon it during the blitz. On one of the pictures from the 1960s we have a view of Park Hill, which when it was built was hailed by sociologists, architects and planners as being one of the country's most significant housing schemes. But then sociologists, planners and architects did not have to live in it. Even though Park Hill won the Department of Environment Design in Housing award in 1967, its residents would soon christen the place San Quentin.

The pictures of Doncaster were taken between 1895 and 1903. The site of the Roman fort of Danum, Doncaster, like Derby, had been transformed by the coming of the railways from an agricultural to an industrial town when it was chosen by the Great Northern Railway as the location for its locomotive and carriage and wagon workshops. Coal mining would also be a major employer with the nearby pits of Brodsworth, Askern Main and Hatfield Main. The early years of the 20th century saw a boom in the opening of new collieries in South Yorkshire. In 1900 the Sheepbridge Coal & Iron Co acquired an interest in the Dinnington Main Coal Co that enabled it to exploit the coalfield to the north of Kiveton Park. The first sod was cut at Brodsworth, near Doncaster, in 1905 and at Hatfield Main on 11th October 1911. The Maltby Main Colliery Co was formed in 1906 with capital of £350,000; in 1912 John Brown & Co and Sheepbridge joined forces to create the Rossington Main Colliery Co to sink a new pit at Rossington. At Hatfield it took five years to reach Barnsley bed coal, struck at a depth of 852yds. Rossington completed sinking in May 1915 and was equipped with plant capable of raising over 5000 tonnes a day.

Among the other places featured in these pages are Askern, Conisbrough, Thorne and Laughton-en-le-Morthen. Askern is situated on the road between Doncaster and Selby, and from the 1820s it enjoyed brief fame as a spa. Its medicinal waters are said to resemble those of Harrogate, and to be efficacious in the treatment of rheumatic and scorbutic disease. A spacious inn was built and many of the villagers offered lodgings. A certain Dr Chorley composed the following: 'The devil when passing through Askeron, Was asked what he thought thereon; Quoth Satan, Judging by the stink, I can't be far from home, I think'.

Conisbrough was once a great royal estate that included the parishes of Dinnington and Laughton-en-le-Morthen. After the Norman Conquest it was held by William de Warenne, whose other South Yorkshire manors included Thorne, Kiveton, Greasbrough and Harthill. The castle with its great cylindrical keep supported by six buttresses was probably built by Henry II's half-brother Hamelin Plantaganet, who had married the last of the Warenne family and took his wife's name. By the mid 16th century Conisbrough was a neglected ruin and was not even garrisoned during the Civil War.

Thorne, once again a manor held by William de Warenne, acquired a new market charter in the 17th century, as did Huddersfield and Penistone. The opening of the Stainforth & Keadby Canal allowed access between the Don and the Trent and brought prosperity to Thorne. By the 1820s there were three shipyards: Ainley & Wardle, Joseph Atkinson & Son and Richard Pearson & Co, as well as ships' victuallers and ship owners. Pearsons may also have been owners. They advertised a weekly sailing from their yard to London and a daily sailing to Sheffield.

Thorne became an important centre for the buying and selling of corn, coal and timber, and developed as an inland port, especially during the second half of the 19th century. The countryside around Thorne is said to resemble Holland rather than Yorkshire, which is just as well, as by 1889 there were over one hundred Dutch immigrants living at Thorne Moorheads. It was the Dutch engineer Vermuyden who was responsible for the cut linking the Don and the Ouse, though most of the immigrants were involved in the peat industry.

Laughton-en-le-Morthen is thought to derive its name from when it was in Danish hands and the local freeholders met in a common assembly to vote on issues affecting themselves. The meeting place has been identified as a hill between the villages of Morthen and Upper Whiston. As early as 1066, when Earl Edwin of Mercia was lord of the manor, it is thought that around 6000 acres were already under cultivation. After the Conquest, Laughton and its rich arable land was held by Roger de Busli (Bully), a major Norman landowner in South Yorkshire, whose other estates included Escafeld (Sheffield), Eclesfeld (Ecclesfield), Mechesburg (Mexborough), Gersebroc (Greasbrough) and Wicresleia (Wickersley).

This book is not an illustrated history of South Yorkshire, but simply a look at the county through the photographs within the Frith archive. However, within these pages we hope you will find one or two interesting snippets of information. For instance: how many did they sleep to the bed in Ecclesfield workhouse? In which shop in Doncaster would middle-class housewives have killed for just to be seen doing their shopping? And why is Nicholas Sanderson of Thurlstone famous?

The last chapter, 'A Day Out In Derbyshire', might seem a little strange, but in the 1880s and 1890s the area was popular with people from Sheffield, thanks in part to the Bank Holidays Act 1871 and the introduction of the Saturday half-day holiday. In the 1880s Baslow had six fair-sized inns owing to its location near the main entrance to Chatsworth House. During the season horse-drawn omnibuses or coaches would leave Sheffield every evening for a trip to Baslow. One route was through Owler Bar, the other by way of Froggatt Edge; the fare on either was 1s 6d. Visitors could also take one or two short walks around the village, either down by the river, or up the hill behind the hydropathic establishment for a look at Chatsworth and the Derwent Valley.

THE CANAL BASIN 1870 S108001

The Sheffield Canal, from the basin to Tinsley, was completed in 1819. It joined the much older Don Navigation and from there went to the Stainforth & Keaby Canal, offering Sheffield manufacturers a link with the navigable River Trent and access to the ports of Hull and Grimsby. In 1905 the newly completed New Junction Canal provided a link between the Don, the Aire & Calder Navigation, and the port of Goole.

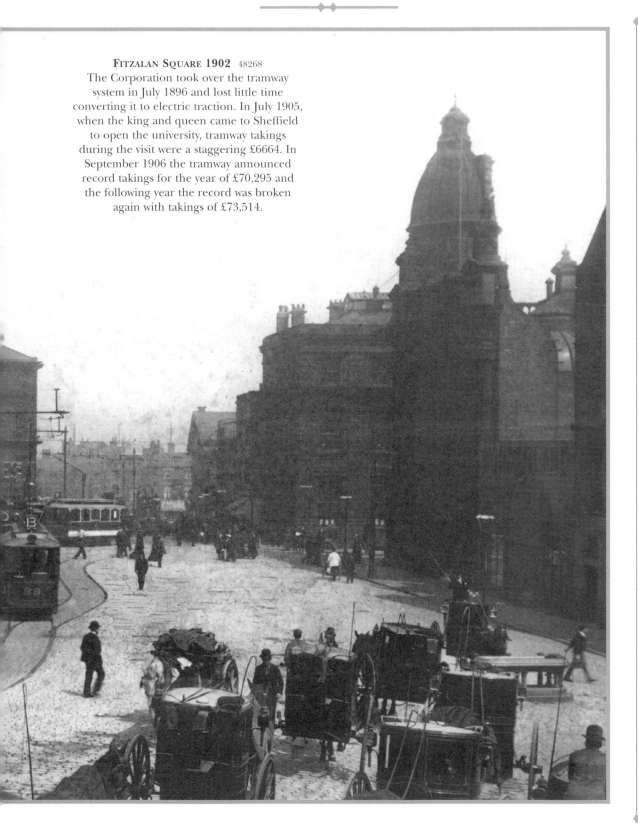

FITZALAN SQUARE 1902 48268
The Corporation took over the tramway
system in July 1896 and lost little time
converting it to electric traction. In July 1905,
when the king and queen came to Sheffield
to open the university, tramway takings
during the visit were a staggering £6664. In
September 1906 the tramway announced
record takings for the year of £70,295 and
the following year the record was broken
again with takings of £73,514.

HIGH STREET 1900 45485
Cabs await their next fares. Fares were set by the local authority: one shilling for the first mile and 6d for each additional half mile. Cabs could also be hired by the hour, the price varying on how many passengers were being carried. For 1-2 persons it was 2s, for 3-4 it was 2s 6d. Between midnight and 6am fares were charged at one and a half times the normal rate.

HIGH STREET c1960 S108110
In the background is the Classic Cinema, which opened as the Electra in 1911. In 1928 the Electra was one of the first cinemas in Sheffield to show part silent, part sound films. Also in the picture is one of the first Atlantean double deckers to be bought by Sheffield Transport Department, the first of which entered service in October 1959.

HIGH STREET c1965 S108175

The High Street was one of the principal shopping areas of the city to be damaged during the air raids of December 1940. The front of the C & A store collapsed into the street following three direct hits, and around seventy people died in the Marples Hotel when it too took a direct hit and was destroyed.

SHEFFIELD MIDLAND STATION c1965 S108222

The Park Hill estate towers above Sheffield Midland station. Hailed by architects, planners and sociologists as being one of the country's most significant housing schemes, Park Hill won the Department of Environment Design in Housing Award in 1967. Vandalism was soon rife and its inhabitants preferred to call it by another name: San Quentin.

THE PARISH CHURCH 1893 31963

THE PARISH CHURCH 1893

The original parish church of St Peter & St Paul was built in the 12th century and rebuilt two or three hundred years later. It is famed for its Shrewsbury Chapel, which is located on the south side of the 15th-century chancel; among the monuments is one to the 6th Earl who was burdened for so many years with the task of looking after Mary, Queen of Scots.

◆

THE CATHEDRAL c1955

In January 1898 the Privy Council gave its approval for Sheffield to have its own Bishopric. However, a few months later the Archbishop of York ordered the scheme abandoned on the grounds that 'it would not be desirable to proceed for some years to come'. It was not until March 1914 that Dr Hedley Burrows was invested as the first Bishop of Sheffield, being enthroned at the cathedral on 1st May.

THE CATHEDRAL c1955 S108035

FARGATE AND SURREY STREET 1893 31961
The Albany was the only temperance hotel in Sheffield to be mentioned alongside the likes of the Royal Victoria
(rooms from 3s 6d, dinner 5s), the Midland, the Talbot and the Wharncliffe.

FARGATE c1955 S108006
In the mid-1950s Sheffield was one of only a handful of cities that still had faith in its tramway system. As late as
1948 the Corporation secured a £200,000 loan from the Ministry of Transport for 35 new four-wheeled trams
with all-metal bodies and fitted with air brakes, the first of which was delivered in May 1950.

FARGATE c1955 S108005
The Sheffield branch of Thomas Cook & Son is dwarfed by its neighbour, Woodhouses. Back in 1851 Sheffield was one of the towns at the centre of a price-cutting war between the Midland and the Great Northern railway companies for the lucrative passenger traffic associated with the Great Exhibition. The GNR cut the return fare from Sheffield to just 5s; the Midland followed suit, and thanks to Thomas Cook tearing up his written agreement, the latter could reduce the fare to just two or three shillings.

THE CITY HALL c1955 S108015
Designed by E Vincent Harris in the classical style featuring a Corinthian columned entrance, the City Hall was built using Darley Dale stone and completed in 1932. Inside is the Oval Hall, where up to 2800 people can be seated for concerts. The front of the hall still bears the scars of the night during World War Two when a bomb landed to the side of the War Memorial, destroying a static water tank into the bargain.

BARKER'S POOL c1965 S108116
In the centre of the picture is the Gaumont cinema, which opened as the Regent in 1927; to the right is Cole Brothers department store. Also featured is the Sheffield War Memorial, designed by Charles Carus Wilson and unveiled in October 1925.

THE FOUNTAIN c1965 S108173
This view looks towards Barker's Pool, where Sheffield's first reservoir was built in 1434 to collect water from several springs on the hillside above West Bar. In the early 18th century John Goodwin and Robert Littlewood built what was really the town's first real reservoir; Barker's Pool was in fact little more than a pond. The fountain is called the Goodwin Fountain.

THE TOWN HALL 1896 37422

The gabled Renaissance-style Town Hall, built on the corner of Pinstone Street and Surrey Street, was designed by E W Mountford and completed in 1896; its official opening by Queen Victoria took place the following year. The tower is 210 ft high and topped off with a bronze statue of Vulcan. In 1898 the city accountant broke the news to the rate payers that the building had cost over £182,000.

THE TOWN HALL c1955 S108012

This photograph shows The Town Hall from the Peace Garden. In 1973 construction began on the Town Hall extension, a modern office block linked to the rear of the existing building by means of a first-floor bridge.

PINSTONE STREET c1965 S108179

Pinstone Street was laid out in the mid-1870s as part of a major development of Sheffield town centre that saw wide well-planned streets replace a hotch-potch of alleyways, small workshops, stables and so on. The other streets were Surrey Street and Leopold Street.

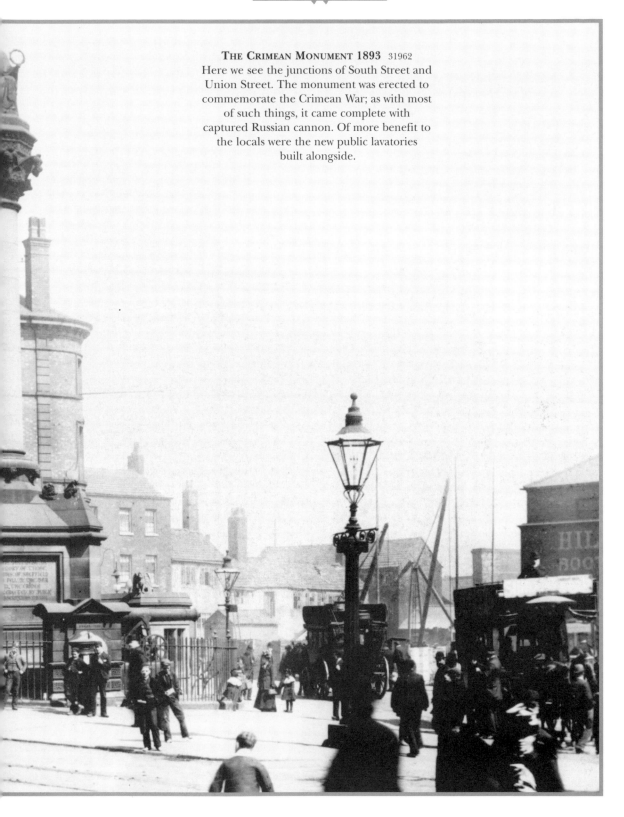

THE CRIMEAN MONUMENT 1893 31962
Here we see the junctions of South Street and
Union Street. The monument was erected to
commemorate the Crimean War; as with most
of such things, it came complete with
captured Russian cannon. Of more benefit to
the locals were the new public lavatories
built alongside.

TRAM TERMINUS c1870 S108002a
The horses usually worked two- to three-hour days, whilst the crews were rostered to work up to 76 hours a week. As early as 1876 the tramway company was seeking an alternative form of traction; it even considered using traction engines to tow the cars along the streets.

THE MOORHEAD c1955 S108002

At around 7.00pm on the evening of 12 December 1940 Sheffield's air raid sirens sounded out their warning over the city. Within a few minutes the first bombs were falling; it was Sheffield's turn to be blitzed. Among the areas hit was the Moor, where many shops and buildings were destroyed or badly damaged, including the large stores belonging to Roberts Brothers and Atkinson's.

THE MOOR c1960 S108087

Post-war reconstruction and redevelopment of the Moor was just one of many schemes to rebuild the city. As well as on commercial and retail developments, a major effort was made on housing. Between 1946-49 the Council built over three thousand new homes, as well as rebuilding others damaged during the blitz.

THE VICTORIA HALL c1955
Situated in Norfolk Street, the Victoria (Methodist) Hall was designed by W F Hale and built in brick with stone dressing. Other Methodist places of worship included a church in Carver Street designed by W Jenkin, who later became a Wesleyan minister himself.

◆

THE POLYTECHNIC c1969
Sheffield Polytechnic was formed in 1969 with the amalgamation of the Sheffield Colleges of Technology and Art; the new institution was housed in purpose-built facilities on land between Howard Street and Pond Street.

THE VICTORIA HALL c1955 S108004

THE POLYTECHNIC c1969 S108221

THE UNIVERSITY C1955 S108049

These are the original university buildings at Western Bank, built between 1903 and 1905. The university was an amalgamation of three earlier institutions, the Sheffield School of Medicine, the Firth College and the Technical School. When the university opened for business in 1905 it had just 100 full-time students.

THE UNIVERSITY C1955 S108046

Following the end of the Second World War, a large number of returning servicemen and women opted for a university education, and by 1947 Sheffield university's student population had more than doubled to 1700. By the mid fifties it was well over 2000.

THE UNIVERSITY c1965 S108181

By the mid-1960s the university had embarked on an ambitious expansion programme complemented with an equally impressive building scheme. The university library is considered to be one of the finest post-Second World War buildings in the city.

WESLEY GRAMMAR SCHOOL 1893 31972

Considered to be somewhat over the top for a school building, this grand edifice with its pedimented centre and end pavilions supported by Corinthian columns was designed by William Flockton and built between 1837-40 as the Wesley Proprietory Grammar School. It was later used by the King Edward VII Grammar School.

HUNTER'S BAR c1965

As Sheffield expanded, a number of turnpike toll bars which had once been in the country were now located within built-up areas. Between 1875 and 1880 the council bought out tolls on the Chesterfield, Langsett and Worksop roads; Hunter's Bar itself was removed on October 1884. The last surviving toll bar in Sheffield was at Meadow Hall - the council paid £1400 for the rights in February 1911.

ECCLESALL, THE CHURCH c1965

Completed in 1789, All Saints' survived in its original form for less than sixty years before it was remodelled and the west tower added. In 1908 the east end of the chancel was extended and the transepts added; the gradient of the site was such that the architect, Temple-Moore, designed a structure supported on a round-arched undercroft.

HUNTER'S BAR c1965 S108224

ECCLESALL, THE CHURCH c1965 S108244

ST GEORGE'S CHURCH 1893 31966

St George's was one of three churches built in
Sheffield between 1825 and 1830 that were
originally district chapels belonging to the
parish church of St Paul's. Sheffield's churches,
chapels and missions ministered not only to the
religious needs of the people, but were often at
the very centre of community life and fulfilled
many of the roles now taken up by the welfare
and social services departments of
local authorities.

NETHER EDGE HOSPITAL c1955 S108081

NETHER EDGE HOSPITAL c1955

In 1930 the Ecclesall Union Hospital came under local government control and was renamed Nether Edge. The institution had an interesting history. When it opened as a workhouse in 1842 there was no segregation of the poor, sick or insane. They were all housed together, and would remain so until 1865, when special wards for infectious diseases and lunatics were established in a new block.

NETHER EDGE ROAD c1955

Around 1955 these three shops provided locals with all manner of things; meat, groceries, sweets, cigarettes, toys and hardware; there was even a lending library. Prices by the mid fifties had doubled on what they had been around 1946: a pound of sirloin cost 4s 2d, 3lb of flour 1s 3d, a dozen eggs would set you back 3s 10d and a pound of butter 2s 6d.

NETHER EDGE ROAD AND POST OFFICE c1955 S108059

NETHER EDGE ROAD c1955 S108064
Nether Edge was one of the residential areas of Sheffield developed during the latter part of the Victorian era and offered a superior standard of housing to that nearer the town centre. As early as 1870, Nether Edge was linked to the town centre by the horse omnibuses owned by the Sharrow Omnibus Co, and in 1899 it was on the first route to be served by electric trams.

BEAUCHIEF, THE ABBEY c1950 B335014
Beauchief is four miles south of Sheffield, but all that remains of the Premonstratensian Abbey founded by Robert Fitz Ranulf around 1183 is the west tower. Around 1662 a small chapel dedicated to St Thomas Beckett was built against the east wall of the tower; many of its fittings including the pulpit, Communion table and box pews date from c1664.

CROOKES VALLEY PARK c1955 S108044
The lake at Crookes Valley Park is in fact one of Sheffield's older reservoirs, converted for use as a boating lake and for fishing. The large building on the left is the reservoir house, part of which was converted for use as a cafe.

CROOKES VALLEY PARK C1955 S108045

It is early morning, and the only activity comes from groundsmen as they go about their tasks. Here we have a view of the cafe and tea garden, the boathouse, bowling green and tennis courts.

MAPPIN ART GALLERY 1893 31968

Weston Park also houses the City Museum and the Mappin Art Gallery. The museum contains a collection of cutlery dating from the 16th century and the world's finest collection of Sheffield plate. As well as hosting a permanent collection of British art, the Mappin also displays loan exhibitions from the extensive collection belonging to the Graves Art Gallery.

ELLIOT'S STATUE 1893 31970a

Born at Masbrough in 1781, the poet Ebenezer Elliot moved to Sheffield following the failure of his father's business. Elliot is famous for his Corn Law Rhymes - he considered the Corn Laws to be an obscenity - but he also composed verses about Sheffield and the surrounding townships. His statue formerly stood in the Market Place.

WESTON PARK C1955 S108128

For a couple of decades or so Sheffield's public parks became the focal point for local Whit-Sunday celebrations. It became something of a tradition on Whit-Sunday for workers and their families to dress up in their best (often their only clothes other than those for work), and make their way to one of the parks where they could join in community hymn singing.

WESTON PARK MEMORIAL C1955 S108039

Weston House and its grounds were sold by the Harrison family to the Corporation in 1873, the house itself being converted into a museum; the Mappin Art Gallery was added in 1887. The war memorial is dedicated to the officers and men of the York & Lancaster Regiment and was unveiled in 1922.

THE BOTANICAL GARDENS 1893 31974
Though the Gardens were opened in
1836, within four years of this picture
being taken the Gardens' operating
company was in financial trouble. The
Town Trustees agreed to buy the
Gardens for £5445 and it was they who
undertook a series of improvements.

THE BOTANICAL GARDENS 1900 45488
Two new plant houses were built in 1900, and in 1903 over £2000 was spent on refurbishing the conservatories, terraces and shed. The three large conservatories designed by B B Taylor were seriously damaged during the Second World War but were eventually restored to their former glory. In 1951 the Gardens were leased to the corporation for a nominal amount.

THE BOTANICAL GARDENS 1900 45492
In 1901 the lady mayoress asked the Trustees if she could use the Gardens for entertainments for children from local workhouses, orphanages and charitable institutions, to celebrate the coronation of King Edward VII. The Trustees agreed and the Gardens were closed to the public on the day.

ENDCLIFFE WOODS 1893

In 1893 the Council controlled five parks. Weston Park was purchased in 1873 for £18,000; Firth Park was given by Mark Firth in 1875; Endcliffe Woods was bought in 1885, followed by Meersbrook Park in 1886 and Hillsborough Park in 1890.

ENDCLIFFE WOODS 1900

It was not until 1920 that the Corporation allowed band concerts in its parks on Sundays; they were light years behind many other towns and cities. Hymn singing in Sheffield's public parks was allowed on Whit Sundays, and in 1912 a special dispensation was granted for a memorial concert in aid of the Titanic Disaster Fund.

ENDCLIFFE WOODS 1893 31977

ENDCLIFFE WOODS 1900 45489

ENDCLIFFE WOODS 1893 31975
Public access to Endcliffe Woods
was extended in 1887 when an
additional nine acres were
purchased through public
subscription and presented to the
town in celebration of Queen
Victoria's golden jubilee. A further
parcel of land was acquired
in 1927.

ENDCLIFFE WOODS 1900 45490

ENDCLIFFE WOODS 1900

The stone gateposts of Hunter's Bar (see picture No S108224) had a second career after the toll bar was finally closed in October 1884; they were resited at the entrance to Endcliffe Park. They remained at Endcliffe until removed to make way for a road improvement scheme and were re-erected at Hunter's Bar.

WIRE MILL DAM c1955

Porter Brook meanders its way from Forge Dam and skirts one edge of Whiteley Woods and Bingham Park before descending over the weirs into Endcliffe Wood. Where the brook flows between Ivy Cottage Lane and Whiteley Wood Road are the walks along the side of Wire Mill Dam.

WIRE MILL DAM c1955 S108028

NORFOLK PARK AVENUE 1893 31973

Owned by the Duke of Norfolk, the 52 acres of Norfolk Park had been open to the citizens of Sheffield since 1841. In 1909 his Grace generously presented the park, then valued at £60,000, to the corporation in perpetuity.

RUSKIN MUSEUM 1893 31971

In 1890 the John Ruskin Museum relocated from a house at Walkley to Meersbrook House in Meersbrook Park. The Museum housed a collection of fine art, drawings, rare books and geological specimens aimed at awakening an appreciation of art in Sheffield's skilled tradesmen. By 1953 the museum was attracting only a handful of visitors a day and the decision was taken to close it.

WHIRLOW BROOK PARK c1955 S108070

WHIRLOW BROOK PARK c1955

Whirlow Brook House was formerly the home of Sir Walter Benton Jones. In 1946 a joint effort by the Town Trust and the J G Graves Charitable Trust secured the grounds for use as a public park. The house itself became a restaurant.

◆

BEAUCHIEF GARDENS c1955

Beauchief Gardens are off Abbeydale Road between Ladies Spring Wood and the Abbeydale Industrial Hamlet. In the background is the former Midland Railway main line between Dore & Totley and Sheffield Midland station. Beauchief once had its own railway station. Originally called Abbey Houses, it was renamed Beauchief in 1870, and became Beauchieff & Abbey Dale in 1874, Beauchief & Abbey Dale in 1889 and Beauchief in 1914. It closed completely in June 1964.

BEAUCHIEF GARDENS c1955 S108090

RIVELIN VALLEY C1955 S108054

In 1899 the council took the decision to acquire the Rivelin Valley and made a number of purchases of land over the coming years. In 1921 the estate covered 245 acres, of which 194 were scheduled for a variety of uses including parkland, housing schemes, allotments and so on. Tenants of the allotments were not allowed to tend to their vegetables on Sundays.

RIVELIN DAM C1955 S108038

In September 1909 the 7623yds long Rivelin Tunnel was completed at a cost of £150,000. It took five years to build with workmen tunnelling from both ends; it carried water from the Derwent Valley to the reservoir at Rivelin.

ECCLESFIELD, GENERAL VIEW 1902 48937
Situated five miles north of Sheffield, the large parish of Ecclesfield was semi-industrialised by the late 18th century. It even had its own workhouse, though it was not unusual for several parishes to club together and operate one between them. This particular establishment was run by a contractor who was paid a set fee per inmate. In 1797 there were 64 parishioners in the workhouse, mainly old people and children. There were 5-6 beds to each room with 2-3 persons per bed. Each bed was provided with two sheets, a blanket and a rug.

ECCLESFIELD, GENERAL VIEW 1902 48936a
By 1821 the population of the parish was over 7000. The Reverend James Dixon was the vicar and Matthew
Spilling the local surgeon, while his wife Ann ran a ladies' boarding school. Sarah Springer was in charge of the
pints at the George & Dragon; Robert Heaton was the governor of the workhouse; and Hannah Hasland
combined running a grocery shop with a drapers. The locals were employed as nail makers, file manufacturers,
flax dressers and linen manufacturers, and Mathew Jepson was the local cooper.

OUGHTIBRIDGE, ONESACRE FROM THE CHURCH c1960 O50030
The view over towards Top Hill Farm, Onesacre Hall, Coldwell and Cold Well Farm.

GRENOSIDE, PROUDLY BRIDGE 1897 40689
Five miles north of Sheffield, Grenoside retained its rural character despite the heavy industry to the west along the banks of the Don and to the east at Ecclesfield.

WORTLEY 1904 53137a
Five miles south-east of Penistone, Wortley was a heavily wooded area famed for its beauty, where Sir Thomas Wortley erected a summer house in 1510. The house was rebuilt in 1743 and again during the early Victorian period. There are a number of monuments to members of the Wortley family in St Leonard's church.

PENISTONE, HIGH STREET C1960 P154004

It was not always quiet on the streets of Penistone; until 1910 cattle and sheep were sold in the streets on Thursdays, and many a deal was struck over a pint or two at the Spread Eagle Hotel. The town's original charter allowed for a weekly market to be held every Tuesday, but for some reason it was allowed to lapse.

PENISTONE, THE SPREAD EAGLE HOTEL C1960 P154003

In 1698 the locals decided to revive Penistone's market day and applied for a new charter. However, there was strong opposition to the proposal from both Barnsley and Huddersfield. A deal was struck with Barnsley whereby they would withdraw their opposition if Penistone opted for a Thursday market.

PENISTONE, THE SHOPPING CENTRE c1960 P154007

PENISTONE
The Shopping Centre c1960
Here we see the changing face of the Co-op. From its humble origins in 1840s Rochdale when two dozen Owenite and Chartist workmen had clubbed together to open a store in T'owd Lane, the movement had become nationwide by the end of the 19th century. The aim was the sale of goods at market prices; what would have been the retailer's profit was divided between the membership in proportion to their purchases - better known to most of us as divi day.

THURLESTONE
The Post Office c1965
One famous 18th century villager was Nicholas Sanderson. As a child Nicholas contracted smallpox which left him blind, yet he learnt to read by passing his fingers over gravestones in the churchyard. His retentive memory must have been outstanding; he learnt Latin and Greek and became a specialist at algebra. He later became professor of mathematics at Cambridge.

THURLESTONE, THE POST OFFICE c1965 T133001

ROYSTON, MIDLAND ROAD c1955 R248001

In the mid-1950s Royston still appears to be a place of cloth caps and head-scarves, and apart from a handful of little differences we could just as easily be looking at Royston in the mid-1930s. The man walking across the road appears oblivious to the oncoming cyclist, and our cameraman is no better: he stood in the middle of the road to get this shot.

BARNSLEY, THE TOWN CENTRE c1950 B333002
The Town Hall dates from 1932-33, designed by Briggs & Thornley and built of Portland stone. On the left is the post office: back in 1822, when Charles Greaves was post-master, it cost a small fortune to send a letter. The rates varied according to distance; 5d to Leeds, 4d to Sheffield, 6d to Chesterfield and 11d to London.

BARNSLEY, THE TOWN HALL c1948 B333005
Barnsley was founded by the monks of St
John's Priory, Pontefract, after they had been
granted the manor and rights to hold weekly
markets and annual fairs. By the early 19th
century Barnsley was a flourishing town of
around 8000 people. There were a couple of
foundries and several coal mines operating,
but many still earned a living working with
flax or bleaching and weaving linen.

BARNSLEY, THE BUS STATION c1955 B333037

In 1955 home car sales passed the 500,000 mark for the first time, but most people relied on buses or trains for getting around. In an earlier age Barnsley was served by stagecoach services to and from London, Leeds, Sheffield and Doncaster. Carriers like Edward Ridsdale operated waggons throughout Yorkshire and offered a freight forwarding service to anywhere within the UK, and Pearson & Co operated a comprehensive packet service on the Barnsley Canal to places such as Hull, Wakefield, Selby, Thorne, York and Gainsboro'.

ASKERN, THE LAKE c1955 A133001

Askern is seven miles north of Doncaster. For a few brief years in the early 19th century it was a spa; its strong sulphuretted medicinal waters were said to resemble those of Harrogate.

THORNE, KING STREET c1965 T303024

Thorne was already a busy market town when the Stainforth & Keadby Canal opened in 1802. The canal provided a link between the navigable rivers Trent and Don, and with its opening Thorne went on to enjoy a new lease of life as an inland port.

THORNE, MARKET PLACE c1965 T303038

At nearby Fishlake, the village church is noted for its late Norman doorway. At Thorne the church of St Nicholas has a late 13th-century tower and early 20th-century glass. The White Hart was once a posting house from which stagecoaches made daily runs to Hull, Doncaster and Sheffield.

BENTLEY, THE RECREATION GROUND c1965 B336003

BENTLEY
The Recreation Ground c1965

We're not sure what our photographer was doing in Bentley: the children playing on the copper's helmet are all well and good, but the photograph was unlikely to make Frith's fortune. According to Pevsner, the architectural marvel at Bentley (which our man failed to photograph) was the pithead baths at the local colliery; these ranked alongside those at Frickley and Manvers Main.

DONCASTER
St George's Church 1900

St George's is considered to be one of Sir Gilbert Scott's finest designs, and was built in 1854-58 as a replacement for the original parish church which had been destroyed by fire. There is a local story that as the old church burned the vicar suddenly exclaimed: 'Good gracious, and I have left my false teeth in the vestry!'

DONCASTER, ST GEORGE'S CHURCH 1900 45111

DONCASTER
Keel Boats On The Don 1903

Despite their cumbersome looks, Humber keel boats carried up to fifty tonnes of cargo, were extremely manoeuvrable, could sail close to the wind, and could be handled by one man. Their origins are obscure, but their rig suggests a direct descent from the Viking trading vessels that once plied the Humber, Ouse, Don and Trent.

◆

DONCASTER
Frenchgate 1903

This view looks south. On the left we have Porter & Sons, wholesale glass and china merchants, and the imposing bulk of the Guildhall with its porticoed entrance supported on Corinthian columns. Many of the buildings on the right hand side of Frenchgate were demolished in the 1960s to make way for the Arndale Centre.

DONCASTER, KEEL BOATS ON THE DON 1903 49857a

DONCASTER, FRENCHGATE 1903 49852

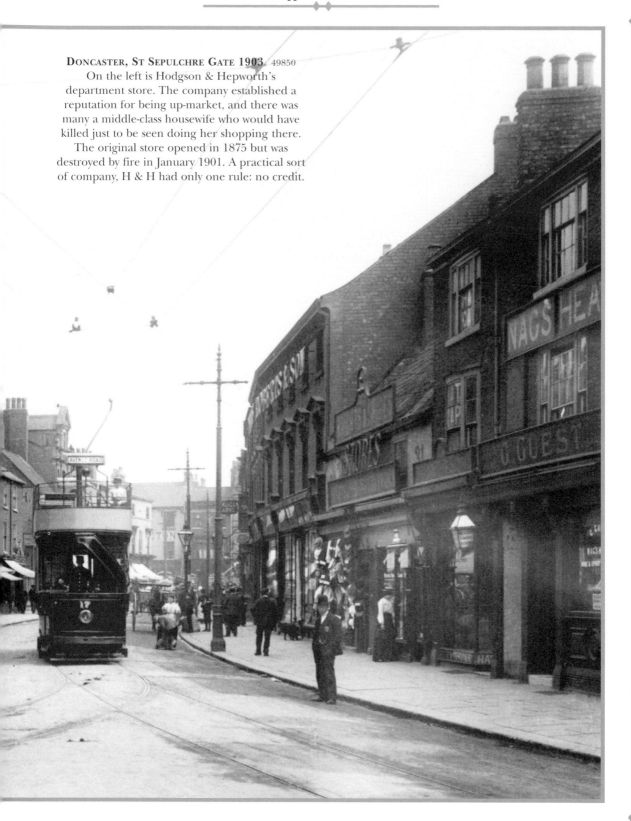

DONCASTER, ST SEPULCHRE GATE 1903 49850
On the left is Hodgson & Hepworth's department store. The company established a reputation for being up-market, and there was many a middle-class housewife who would have killed just to be seen doing her shopping there.

The original store opened in 1875 but was destroyed by fire in January 1901. A practical sort of company, H & H had only one rule: no credit.

DONCASTER, BAXTERGATE 1903 49853
Here we see Baxtergate at the junction of St Sepulchre Gate and the High Street. It was down Baxtergate that
Freeman, Hardy & Willis had their branch, and where those who had signed the pledge could find a room at the
Albany Temperance Hotel.

DONCASTER, HIGH STREET 1895 35313a
Had this picture been taken a few months earlier, Doncaster's then second most familiar landmark after St George's would have been captured on camera. Clock Corner, so called because of the huge clock visible the length of the street, would have been in the background on the right hand side. It was demolished in 1894.

DONCASTER, STATION ROAD 1903 49854
The Doncaster Mutual Co-operative Society is on the left of the picture, and Glyn's Temperance Hotel is immediately behind the tram. Had our man from Frith turned his camera to the left he would have photographed Theobald & Son the basket makers, and what would become to be known as the Red House; outside here, meetings were often held in the street with arresting results.

DONCASTER, HIGH STREET 1903 49851a
Doncaster's electric street tramway opened in 1902 and lasted until 1935, when trolley buses took over. Other tramway systems closing that year included Aberdare, Burnley, Darwen, Erith, Norwich, Preston, Warrington and the short-lived system at York.

DONCASTER, CHRIST CHURCH 1893 31987
Christ Church in Thorne Road was opened in 1829. Designed by William Hurst, it is noted for its Belgian glass and a steeple that features an octagonal lantern.

DONCASTER, THE GRANDSTAND 1903 49856
By the date this picture was taken, Doncaster had been a racing centre for nearly three hundred years and had been the home of the oldest classic race, the St Leger, since its first running in 1778. The earliest grandstand was designed by John Carr of York and dates from 1776. Carr's other work includes the Crescent (1780-84) and the Great Stables (1789) at Buxton, Derbyshire, commissioned by the fifth Duke of Devonshire after seeing some of Carr's work at Wentworth Woodhouse, seat of Lord Rockingham.

SPROTBROUGH, THE CANAL BRIDGE 1895 35328
It is said that Sprotbrough once welcomed strangers. There used to be a cross with a brass plate on it on which the following was inscribed: 'Whoso is hungry, and lists well to eat, Let him come to Sprotbrough, for his meat, And for a night and for a day, His horse shall have both corn and hay, And none shall ask him when he goes away'.

SPROTBROUGH, ST MARY'S CHURCH 1895 35325
The church dates mainly from the late 13th century, though the west tower is later; in 1474 William Fitzherbert left £40 in his will towards construction costs. In the chancel is an old stone seat, thought to be a sanctuary chair, and a brass of William Fitzherbert and his wife.

SPROTBROUGH, THE HALL 1900 45304

By the 1650s Lionel Copley had become one of the leading ironmasters in South Yorkshire, thanks to a leasing arrangement with the Earl of Shrewsbury which gave him access to Shrewsbury charcoal woods and coal and ironstone pits. The Copley family prospered, and Sprotbrough Hall was built by Sir Godfrey Copley. It was demolished in 1926.

CONISBROUGH, THE CASTLE 1895 35317A

Conisbrough is derived from Cyningsburgh, Anglo-Saxon for the king's fortified settlement; it features in Sir Walter Scott's novel 'Ivanhoe' as the home of Athelstan, the last of the Saxon royal line. Work on replacing the original wooden castle with one of masonry is thought to have been started by Hamelin Plantaganet, half-brother of Henry II.

CONISBROUGH, THE CASTLE 1895 35318

CONISBROUGH
The Castle 1895
Built out of the local creamy-white limestone, the keep is 90 ft high and has six semi-hexagonal buttresses which rise above it to form mini-turrets. By the mid 16th century the castle was semi-derelict: a long stretch of curtain wall had collapsed and at least one floor of the keep had fallen in. The fortress was in such poor condition that it was never garrisoned during the Civil War.

◆

CONISBROUGH
The Church 1895
Though St Peter's dates from Saxon times, it is believed that Hamelin Plantaganet might have also have rebuilt the church, as much of the stonework is 12th-century. The most important feature is a carved Norman tomb-chest depicting various scenes including knights jousting, Adam and Eve, and a warrior fighting with a dragon.

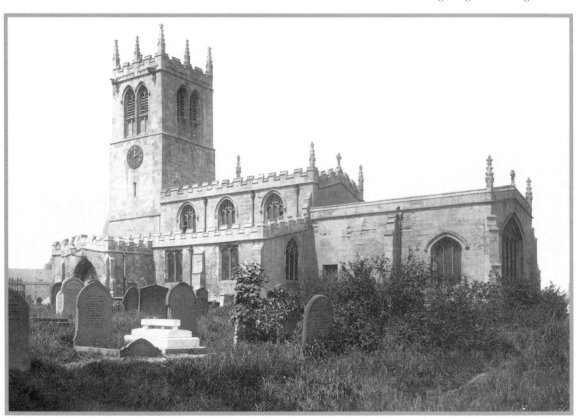

CONISBROUGH, THE CHURCH 1895 35322

GREASBROUGH c1965 G111004
The skyline is dominated by the pinnacled tower of St Mary's church, built in 1826 to the designs of Charles Watson and J P Pritchett. The font cover is Jacobean, and once belonged to All Saints', Rotherham.

GREASBROUGH c1965 G111006
Greasbrough was once described as a pleasant village 'situated on a delightful eminence'; by the early 19th century it was a farming and mining community of over 1000. In 1821 there were at least three inns, the Yellow Lion, the King's Head and the Queen's Head.

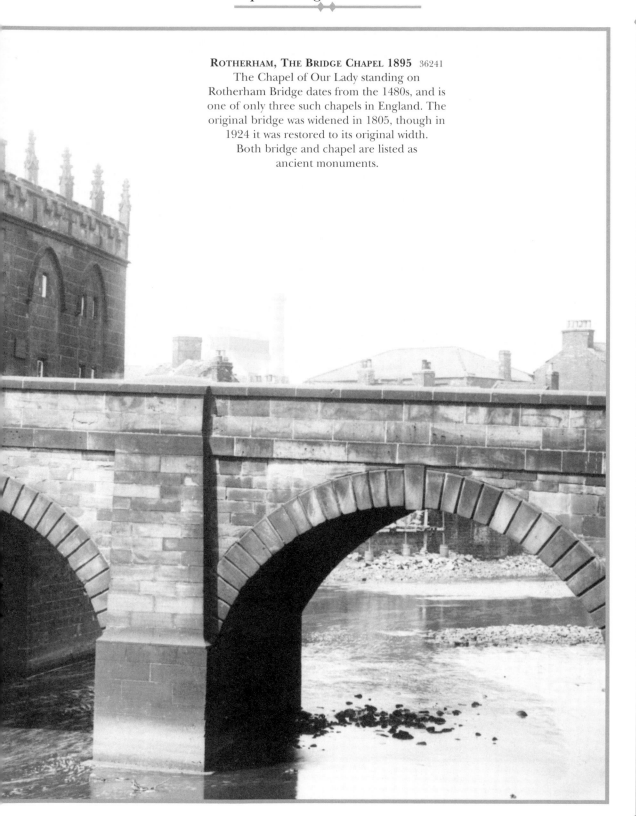

ROTHERHAM, THE BRIDGE CHAPEL 1895 36241
The Chapel of Our Lady standing on
Rotherham Bridge dates from the 1480s, and is
one of only three such chapels in England. The
original bridge was widened in 1805, though in
1924 it was restored to its original width.
Both bridge and chapel are listed as
ancient monuments.

ROTHERHAM, CLIFTON PARK 1895   36244

ROTHERHAM
Clifton Park 1895

Clifton House, which is now the local museum, dates from 1782 and is the work of John Carr of York, one of the country's outstanding architects of his day. It was built for Joshua Walker, the son of Rotherham ironmaster and leading Nonconformist Samuel Walker.

◆

ROTHERHAM
Town Centre 1961

This photograph was taken from All Saints' Church, itself one of the finest examples of Perpendicular architecture in Yorkshire. In the background is the Old College Hotel, a name that echoes back to the founding of the College of Jesus by the Archbishop of York in 1500. For a few brief years Rotherham became a centre of learning, until the college was closed during the Dissolution.

ROTHERHAM, TOWN CENTRE 1961   R60042

ROTHERHAM

The Grammar School 1957

Rotherham Grammar School grew out of a free school that had been endowed through royal patronage. But the days of grammar school education were numbered: the incoming Labour Government in 1964 championed the amalgamation of grammar and secondary modern schools into comprehensives, the theory being that all pupils would have a chance to succeed academically.

◆

MALTBY

High Street c1955

Despite being an ancient settlement, Maltby was still little more than a village at the beginning of the 20th century. Then things changed. In 1902 the Sheepbridge Coal & Iron Co leased land from the Earl of Scarbrough, and in 1906 the Maltby Main Colliery Co was formed. At its height the colliery employed several thousand miners, and Maltby's population rose to over 15,000.

ROTHERHAM, THE GRAMMAR SCHOOL 1957 R60017

MALTBY, HIGH STREET c1955 M140009

MALTBY, HIGH STREET c1955 M140005
It is sale time again at Maltby's local department store, G T Thompson's. Here locals could spend their money on furniture, boots and shoes, children's clothes, and ladies' and gents' outfitting.

MALTBY, THE PARISH CHURCH c1955 M140018
Though the west tower with its distinctive recessed spire is said to contain masonry older than Roche Abbey, the rest of St Bartholomew's dates from 1859, when it was rebuilt to a design by P Boyce. Maltby is one of four West Riding settlements credited in the Domesday survey with having four mills; the others are Tanshelf, Dadsley and Kippax.

MALTBY
Manor Road c1955
Manor Road would not win any architectural awards; in fact, the picture could have been taken in any one of a hundred or so towns where similar houses were built. The architectural highlight of the town as far as Pevsner was concerned was the pithead baths at Maltby Main, designed by W A Woodland and built in 1938.

◆

MALTBY
The Crossroads c1965
BBC and ITV aerials proliferate above the rooftops of Maltby. Also featured is Blackham's supermarket; after all, this was in the days when there was no such thing as out-of-town retail centres, and the only connection the word 'convenience' had with shopping was in spending a penny.

MALTBY, MANOR ROAD c1955 M140004

MALTBY, THE CROSSROADS c1965 M140022

WICKERSLEY, ST ALBAN'S CHURCH c1955 W228001

WICKERSLEY
St Alban's Church c1955

Wickersley is four miles east of Rotherham. Its people once earned their livings making grind stones, around 5000 a year in the 1820s, in varying diameters from one to six feet. Business must have been good, because there was enough money around in 1834 for the church to be given a new nave. The chancel dates from 1886, and the stained glass is also vintage 1880s.

◆

WICKERSLEY
Royds Moor c1955

A royd is a northern name for an assart, a practice going back to medieval times when the population of a hamlet cleared land, usually sufficient to make one or two fields, for crops. They would sow oats in spring which were harvested late, followed by a winter crop of rye. Royds Moor is named after a royd cleared for crops probably around the mid 12th century.

WICKERSLEY, ROYDS MOOR c1955 W228003

WHISTON, THE POST OFFICE c1955 W226021

Two miles south east of Rotherham, Whiston was a large village by the end of the Napoleonic Wars. By 1821 the population had passed the 850 mark; the church had both a rector (Rev Richard Lacy) and a curate (Rev Benjamin Birkitt). As well as village constable, blacksmith, and millwright, there was a collector of taxes and a collector of rates. J & W Heward ran a tannery, James White was a maltster and Richard Cutt a linen manufacturer.

TICKHILL, MARKET PLACE c1955 T136003

Situated nine miles east of Rotherham on the A361, the village of Tickhill once had one of the most important castles in the North, built on a motte no less than 75ft high and surrounded by a wet moat 30ft wide. The original castle was built of wood, but it was replaced with stone in the early 12th century, probably by Henry I after he had confiscated the fortress from Robert de Belleme.

TICKHILL, MARKET PLACE c1955 T136002
When this picture was taken Tickhill was in a West Riding mining area, but it had retained its rural image and appeal. As well as the castle, the parish church of St Mary's is considered to be one of the finest in Yorkshire, having been rebuilt in white magnesian limestone in the late 14th century, though some earlier parts still remain. Among the treasures are the tomb-chest of Thomas Fitzwilliam (died 1478), a late 15th-century font, and an early 17th-century pulpit.

ROCHE ABBEY 1893 31978
Founded in 1147, Roche Abbey was a colony of Newminster in Northumberland, itself
a daughter of the great Cistercian abbey of Fountains. The abbey took its name from
a cross-like rock that was already an object of pilgrimage for the faithful. The main
ruins comprise parts of the east walls of the transepts, part of the chancel and a
vaulted gatehouse.

ROCHE ABBEY 1893 31979

In 1538 Roche Abbey was surrendered to the Crown and destroyed. The choir stalls were fired to melt lead; timber and stone were sold off as the great building was reduced to little more than a quarry. Michael Sherbrook, rector of Wickersley, wrote: 'All things of price either spoiled, carted away, or defaced to the uttermost.....nothing was spared but the oxhouses and swinecoates and other such houses of office, that stood without the walls'.

LAUGHTON-EN-LE-MORTHEN, ALL SAINTS' CHURCH c1965 L526001

Just 2.25 miles south-west of Roche Abbey stands All Saints'. Its fine Perpendicular spire is unusual, in that the corner walling of the belfry is sloped off. It is also one of several churches where the architect has employed toy flying buttresses; other examples are St Mary's, Whittlesea and King's Sutton, Northants.

DINNINGTON
The Square c1965

The independent parish of Dinnington almost cuts the parish of Laughton-en-le-Morthen in two. In the mid 11th century Dinnington was still a part of the old royal estate of Conisbrough, along with Harthill, Braithwell and Anston, though Laughton had been detached and was ruled by Earl Edwin of Mercia.

DINNINGTON
Lordens Hill c1965

This photograph shows Lordens Hill on a somewhat gloomy day. There are few cars parked along the street, but in those days private car ownership amid working families was still something of a novelty. The average wage was around £17 a week, and the annual road fund licence was £17.10.0d. A new Ford Cortina saloon cost £669, and a Zephyr £933.

DINNINGTON, THE SQUARE c1965 D101012

DINNINGTON, LORDENS HILL c1965 D101008

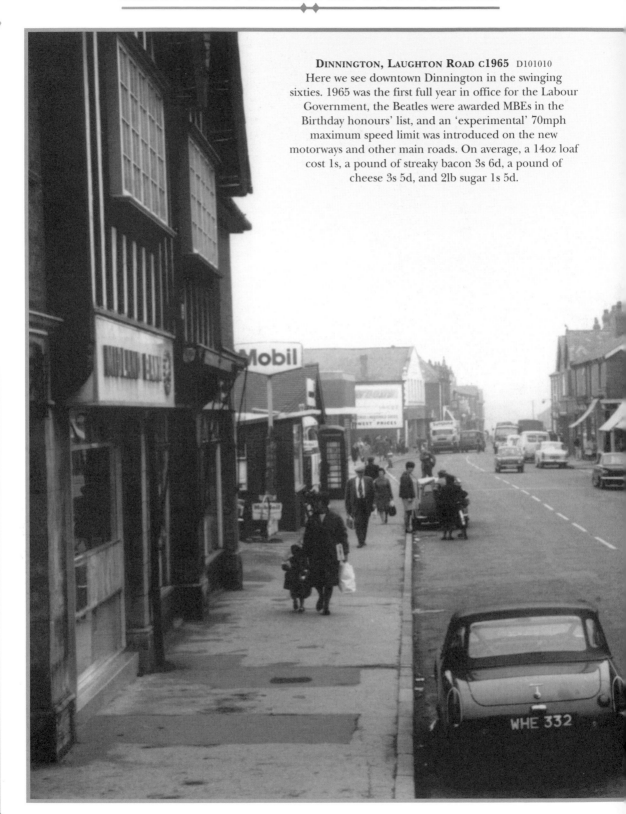

DINNINGTON, LAUGHTON ROAD c1965 D101010
Here we see downtown Dinnington in the swinging sixties. 1965 was the first full year in office for the Labour Government, the Beatles were awarded MBEs in the Birthday honours' list, and an 'experimental' 70mph maximum speed limit was introduced on the new motorways and other main roads. On average, a 14oz loaf cost 1s, a pound of streaky bacon 3s 6d, a pound of cheese 3s 5d, and 2lb sugar 1s 5d.

NORTH ANSTON, CROWGATE c1960 A126018
After the Norman Conquest, the lands belonging to those theyns who had either fought for Harold or were implicated in the Northern rebellions were confiscated and awarded to William's followers. One powerful Norman lord in South Yorkshire was Roger de Bully. His estates included North Anston, Greasbrough, Wickersley, Ecclesfield, Laughton-en-le-Morthen and Mexborough.

KIVETON PARK, THE METHODIST CHURCH c1965 K81002
Kiveton Park was once an estate belonging to Sir Thomas Osborne, Earl of Danby and later First Duke of Leeds; the house, designed by William Talman, has long since been demolished. In 1900 the Sheepbridge Coal & Iron Co secured an interest in the Dinnington Main Coal Co, which had been formed to exploit the coalfield to the north of Kiveton Park.

WALES, CHURCH STREET c1955 W519007a
The village of Wales lies seven miles south of Rotherham in the wapentake of Strafforth and Tickhill. A wapentake is an old Danelaw administrative area, and harks back to a time when all freeholding landowners within the district had the right to attend and vote at council meetings. Each man entitled to vote did so by raising his sword, hence wapentake - the counting of the weapons.

WALES, MANOR ROAD c1955 W519003

At the beginning of the 11th century Wales, the 'territory of the Welshmen', was owned by the wealthy Mercian thegn Wulfric Spott, who also owned lands in Derbyshire and Staffordshire. By 1066 Spott's former lands around Wales had been divided into several manors with scattered blocks of land.

WALES, THE SQUARE c1955 W519009

Farm buildings in the heart of the village bear testimony to a time when most villagers worked on the land. In the days when the Reverend William Downes was rector, and William Wilkinson kept the Leeds Arms, local farmers included Joseph Booth, Jonathan Marshall, Maude Thomas, John Shirt and Thomas Stanland.

WALES
The Church c1955
The church of St John Baptist dates back to Norman times, when it consisted of a west tower, nave and chancel. In 1897 the building was extended so that the original Norman structure formed the north aisle, and a new nave and south aisle were built.

◆

HARTHILL
The Church c1955
The earliest parts of All Hallows date from c1200; the chancel is 13th century, and Victorian additions include the east window and north aisle windows. Some of the stained glass is from Florence. The monuments to Lady Margaret Osborne and the First Duke of Leeds are of outstanding quality and craftsmanship.

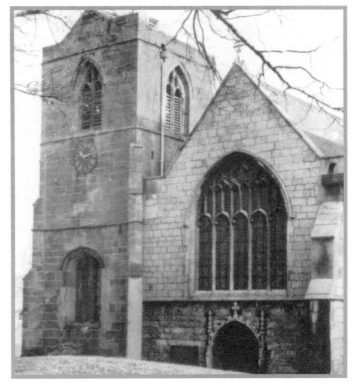

WALES, THE CHURCH c1955 W519013

HARTHILL, THE CHURCH c1955 H139009

HARTHILL, WOODHALL LANE c1965 H139019
When this picture was taken there had been a Blue
Bell inn in the village for over 140 years. In the early
1820s the village had three inns. The Blue Bell was
kept by F Glossop, who was also a maltster; the
landlord at the White Hart was Thomas Booth; and
William Clark ran the Three Crowns. The village also
had a surgeon (George Frith) and a constable
(George Brunt).

BASLOW
The Hydropathic Establishment 1886
Finely situated on the brow of a hill to the north-east of the village, the hydro offered guests the usual water treatments and dietary regimes. The hydro operated its own coach and four to Sheffield and back several days a week.

BASLOW
The Old Mill 1886
Here we see the old bridge and the mill. A guide book for 1886 states that the village had no special feature of interest to the tourist, though its situation was pleasant and that the church with its stumpy spire was charmingly placed amid a grove of lime trees.

BASLOW, THE HYDROPATHIC ESTABLISHMENT 1886   16582

BASLOW, THE BRIDGE 1886   16576

CHATSWORTH, CHATSWORTH HOUSE 1886 18643

The house was begun by William Cavendish, fourth Earl and later first Duke of Devonshire, in 1687 and completed in 1706; the north wing was added between 1820-30. Royalties from the Ecton Copper Mine in the Manifold Valley enabled the house to be furnished on a lavish scale. Between 1760 and 1817 the profits from Ecton were in excess of £335,000. In 1886 the house was open to the public from 11.00am to 4.00pm during the week, and from 11.00am to 1.00pm on Saturdays. Admission was free.

HADDON HALL 1886 18630

Haddon Hall survives as one of the finest examples of a 16th and 17th century residence owing to the fact that when the Duke of Rutland abandoned it in favour of Belvoir Castle in 1700, it was not allowed to fall into a state of disrepair. Haddon is also the scene of a classic love story. Dorothy Vernon, second daughter of Sir George, was betrothed to Edward Stanley, younger son of the Earl of Derby. But Dorothy loved John Manners, younger son of the Earl of Rutland. On the eve of her wedding she slipped away from the ballroom, out of the Hall, and into John's arms. Dorothy and John were married, and later lived at Haddon.

HATHERSAGE, THE VILLAGE 1902 48914

Hathersage in 1902 was just a train ride away from
Sheffield, offering a mixture of fresh air, romance and
legend. The fresh air took care of itself; the romance
was provided by Charlotte Bronte, a glimpse of whom
was enough to make the local rector Henry Nussey
lovesick. The stuff of legend comes from Robin Hood:
Hathersage is said to be the birthplace and burial
place of Robin's friend Little John.

HATHERSAGE, THE VILLAGE 1902 48915a
The main road to Sheffield as it used to look. In the centre of the picture is the George Hotel, an old coaching inn; it has since been completely rebuilt.

HATHERSAGE, THE VILLAGE 1919 69193a
On the left we have the George Hotel in its rebuilt form, complete with battlements. Around this date the village had a population of about 1600; early closing was on a Wednesday and Tuesday was market day.

HATHERSAGE, THE VILLAGE 1902 48917
This view looks towards the village from
the Sheffield road. On the right is the
Ordnance Arms, better known to today's
tourists as the ivy-covered Hathersage
Inn. The small building serving as a bank
is now a three-storey affair.

HATHERSAGE 1919 69201a

This photograph shows the climb out of Hathersage on the Sheffield road near Millstone Edge. Near here is Bole Hill. A bole was a medieval method of smelting lead ore: it was a stone-built affair with an opening toward the prevailing wind, in which layers of timber and ore were placed. When the wind was in the right direction the bole was fired and the lead trickled down into a collecting pool to create a pig.

CASTLETON, SPEEDWELL CAVERN 1909 61785

The caverns at Castleton were, and still are, a popular day out for people from the Sheffield area. Here we have the entrance to the Speedwell Cavern, and Winnats Pass is little more than a track for sheep. Speedwell's history goes back to the 18th century, when a shaft was driven underground in the search for lead ore. The cavern's unique feature is a 750yd underground canal.

CASTLETON, THE MARKET PLACE 1909 61776

Peveril Castle stands on a hill 260ft above the village, yet despite its looks it was far from impregnable; it was even in Scottish hands for a number of years. It was here that Henry II and Malcolm of Scotland reached an agreement to hand Peveril back to the English crown, whereupon Henry had the fortress rebuilt and added a keep.

Index

Frith Book Co 1999 Titles

From 2000 we aim at publishing 100 new books each year. For latest catalogue please contact Frith Book Co

Barnstaple	1-85937-084-5	£12.99	Oct 99		Maidstone	1-85937-056-X	£12.99	Oct 99
Blackpool	1-85937-049-7	£12.99	Oct 99		Northumberland & Tyne and Wear	1-85937-072-1	£14.99	Sep 99
Bognor Regis	1-85937-055-1	£12.99	Oct 99		North Yorkshire	1-85937-048-9	£14.99	Oct 99
Bristol	1-85937-050-0	£12.99	Oct 99		Nottingham	1-85937-060-8	£12.99	Oct 99
Cambridge	1-85937-092-6	£12.99	Nov 99		Oxfordshire	1-85937-076-4	£14.99	Oct 99
Cambridgeshire	1-85937-086-1	£14.99	Nov 99		Penzance	1-85937-069-1	£12.99	Oct 99
Cheshire	1-85937-045-4	£14.99	Oct 99		Reading	1-85937-087-X	£12.99	Nov 99
Chester	1-85937-090-X	£12.99	Nov 99		St Ives	1-85937-068-3	£12.99	Oct 99
Chesterfield	1-85937-071-3	£12.99	Oct 99		Salisbury	1-85937-091-8	£12.99	Nov 99
Chichester	1-85937-089-6	£12.99	Nov 99		Scarborough	1-85937-104-3	£12.99	Oct 99
Cornwall	1-85937-054-3	£14.99	Oct 99		Scottish Castles	1-85937-077-2	£14.99	Nov 99
Cotswolds	1-85937-099-3	£14.99	Nov 99		Sevenoaks and Tonbridge	1-85937-057-8	£12.99	Oct 99
					Sheffield and S Yorkshire	1-85937-070-5	£12.99	Oct 99
					Shropshire	1-85937-083-7	£14.99	Nov 99
					Southampton	1-85937-088-8	£12.99	Nov 99
					Staffordshire	1-85937-047-0	£14.99	Nov 99
					Stratford upon Avon	1-85937-098-5	£12.99	Nov 99
					Suffolk	1-85937-074-8	£14.99	Nov 99
					Surrey	1-85937-081-0	£14.99	Nov 99
					Torbay	1-85937-063-2	£12.99	Oct 99
					Wiltshire	1-85937-053-5	£14.99	Oct 99

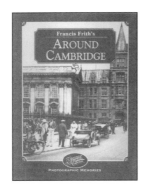

Derby	1-85937-046-2	£12.99	Oct 99
Devon	1-85937-052-7	£14.99	Oct 99
Dorset	1-85937-075-6	£14.99	Oct 99
Dorset Coast	1-85937-062-4	£14.99	Nov 99
Dublin	1-85937-058-6	£12.99	Oct 99
East Anglia	1-85937-059-4	£14.99	Oct 99
Eastbourne	1-85937-061-6	£12.99	Oct 99
English Castles	1-85937-078-0	£14.99	Oct 99
Essex	1-85937-082-9	£14.99	Nov 99
Falmouth	1-85937-066-7	£12.99	Oct 99
Hampshire	1-85937-064-0	£14.99	Nov 99
Hertfordshire	1-85937-079-9	£14.99	Nov 99
Isle of Man	1-85937-065-9	£14.99	Nov 99
Liverpool	1-85937-051-9	£12.99	Sep 99

British Life A Century Ago

246 x 189mm 144pp, hardback. Black and white Lavishly illustrated with photos from the turn of the century, and with extensive commentary. It offers a unique insight into the social history and heritage of bygone Britain.

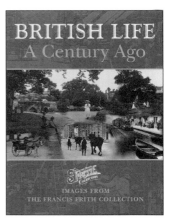

1-85937-103-5 £17.99

Available from your local bookshop or from the publisher

FRITH PRODUCTS & SERVICES

Francis Frith would doubtless be pleased to know that the pioneering publishing venture he started in 1860 still continues today. More than a hundred and thirty years later, The Francis Frith Collection continues in the same innovative tradition and is now one of the foremost publishers of vintage photographs in the world. Some of the current activities include:

Interior Decoration

Today Frith's photographs can be seen framed and as giant wall murals in thousands of pubs, restaurants, hotels, banks, retail stores and other public buildings throughout the country. In every case they enhance the unique local atmosphere of the places they depict and provide reminders of gentler days in an increasingly busy and frenetic world.

Product Promotions

Frith products have been used by many major companies to promote the sales of their own products or to reinforce their own history and heritage. Brands include Hovis bread, Courage beers, Scots Porage Oats, Colman's mustard, Cadbury's foods, Mellow Birds coffee, Dunhill pipe tobacco, Guinness, and Bulmer's Cider.

Genealogy and Family History

As the interest in family history and roots grows world-wide, more and more people are turning to Frith's photographs of Great Britain for images of the towns, villages and streets where their ancestors lived; and, of course, photographs of the churches and chapels where their ancestors were christened, married and buried are an essential part of every genealogy tree and family album.

A series of easy-to-use CD Roms is planned for publication, and an increasing number of Frith photographs will be able to be viewed on specialist genealogy sites. A growing range of Frith books will be available on CD.

The Internet

Already thousands of Frith photographs can be viewed and purchased on the internet. By the end of the year 2000 some 60,000 Frith photographs will be available on the internet. The number of sites is constantly expanding, each focussing on different products and services from the Collection.

Some of the sites are listed below.

www.townpages.co.uk
www.familystorehouse.com
www.britannia.com
www.icollector.com
www.barclaysquare.co.uk
www.cornwall-online.co.uk

For background information on the Collection look at the two following sites:

www.francisfrith.com
www.francisfrith.co.uk

Frith Products

All Frith photographs are available Framed or just as Mounted Prints, and can be ordered from the address below. From time to time other products - Address Books, Calendars, Table Mats, Postcards etc - are available.

The Frith Collectors' Guild

In response to the many customers who enjoy collecting Frith photographs we have created the Frith Collectors' Guild. Members are entitled to a range of benefits, including a regular magazine, special discounts and special limited edition products.

For further information: if you would like further information on any of the above aspects of the Frith business please contact us at the address below:

The Francis Frith Collection, Frith's Barn, Teffont, Salisbury, Wiltshire England SP3 5QP.
Tel: +44 (0) 1722 716 376 Fax: +44 (0) 1722 716 881 Email: frithbook.co.uk

To receive your FREE Mounted Print

Cut out this Voucher and return it with your remittance for £1.50 to cover postage and handling. Choose any photograph included in this book. Your SEPIA print will be A4 in size, and mounted in a cream mount with burgundy rule lines, overall size 14 x 11 inches.

Order additional Mounted Prints at HALF PRICE (only £7.49 each*)

If there are further pictures you would like to order, possibly as gifts for friends and family, acquire them at half price (no additional postage and handling required).

Have your Mounted Prints framed*

For an additional £14.95 per print you can have your chosen Mounted Print framed in an elegant polished wood and gilt moulding, overall size 16 x 13 inches (no additional postage and handling required).

---

* IMPORTANT!
These special prices are only available if ordered using the original voucher on this page (no copies permitted) and at the same time as your free Mounted Print, for delivery to the same address

---

Frith Collectors' Guild

From time to time we publish a magazine of news and stories about Frith photographs and further special offers of Frith products. If you would like 12 months FREE membership, please return this form and we will send you a New Member Pack.

Send completed forms to:
The Francis Frith Collection, Frith's Barn, Teffont, Salisbury, Wiltshire SP3 5QP

Voucher for FREE and Reduced Price Frith Prints

Picture no.	Page number	Qty	Mounted @ £7.49	Framed + £14.95	Total Cost
		1	**Free of charge***	£	£
			£	£	£
			£	£	£
			£	£	£
			£	£	£
			£	£	£

Title: SHEFFIELD & SOUTH YORKSHIRE 070-5

* Post & handling	£1.50
Total Order Cost	£

Please do not photocopy this voucher. Only the original is valid, so please cut it out and return it to us.

I enclose a cheque / postal order for £ . . . . made payable to 'The Francis Frith Collection' OR please debit my Mastercard / Visa / Switch / Amex card

Number . . . .

Expires . . . . Signature . . . .

Name Mr/Mrs/Ms . . . .

Address . . . .

. . . .

. . . .

. . . . Postcode . . . .

Daytime Tel No . . . .   Valid to 31/12/01

The Francis Frith Collectors' Guild

I would like to receive the New Members Pack offering 12 months FREE membership.

070-5

Name Mr/Mrs/Ms . . . .

Address . . . .

. . . .

. . . .

. . . . Postcode . . . .

Free Print - see overleaf